Cryptocurrency

The Ultimate Guide to Investing, Trading, and Mining Cryptocurrency

© Copyright 2017 by Roger Bray - All rights reserved.

The following eBook is reproduced below with the goal of providing information that is as accurate and reliable as possible. Regardless, purchasing this eBook can be seen as consent to the fact that both the publisher and the author of this book are in no way experts on the topics discussed within and that any recommendations or suggestions that are made herein are for entertainment purposes only. Professionals should be consulted as needed prior to undertaking any of the action endorsed herein.

This declaration is deemed fair and valid by both the American Bar Association and the Committee of Publishers Association and is legally binding throughout the United States.

Furthermore, the transmission, duplication or reproduction of any of the following work including specific information will be considered an illegal act irrespective of if it is done electronically or in print. This extends to creating a secondary or tertiary copy of the work or a recorded copy and is only allowed with express written consent from the Publisher. All additional rights reserved.

The information in the following pages is broadly considered to be a truthful and accurate account of facts and as such any inattention, use or misuse of the information in question by the reader will render any resulting actions solely under their purview. There are no scenarios in which the publisher or the original author of this work can be in any fashion deemed liable for any hardship or damages that may befall them after undertaking information described herein.

Additionally, the information in the following pages is intended only for informational purposes and should thus be thought of as universal. As befitting its nature, it is presented without assurance regarding its prolonged validity or interim quality. Trademarks that are mentioned are done without written consent and can in no way be considered an endorsement from the trademark holder.

Table of Contents

Introduction 1

Chapter 1: Investing in Cryptocurrencies 3

Chapter 2: Trading in Cryptocurrency 21

Chapter 3: Mining in Cryptocurrencies 40

Conclusion 57

Introduction

Congratulations on purchasing this book and thank you for doing so.

The following chapters will discuss some of the basics that you need to know to start making some money with cryptocurrencies. While most people are getting into the market in the hopes of doing trades internationally or to keep their information safe from the government or from other people, investing, trading, and mining are all great methods that you can choose to earn some money from all the potential and popularity that comes with these digital currencies.

Inside this guidebook, you will get the best tips to help you make money with cryptocurrencies. We will start with some of the basics of investing in cryptocurrencies and how you should learn how to pick the right strategies and understand the market cycle to see success. We will then move on to trading and how picking the right times to leave the market and keeping your emotions out of the mix will ensure that you trade successfully every time. And finally, mining is another method that you can choose to help you get started with earning coins without having to add in as much risk. That chapter will discuss the hardware and software that you need to start and some other tricks that will make it easier to start.

While others are concentrating on sending money or making purchases with the help of cryptocurrencies, some smart investors see this as a great way to earn a great income. Use this guidebook to give you the tips that you need to get started on your own strategy for making money with cryptocurrencies today.

There are plenty of books on this subject on the market, thanks again for choosing this one! Every effort was made to ensure it is full of as much useful information as possible, please enjoy!

Chapter 1: Investing in Cryptocurrencies

There are a lot of reasons why you would consider joining a cryptocurrency network. Most people choose to join this network because it helps them to do trades between countries without all of the red tape or the fees. Some just like the idea of being able to send money or do other transactions without the government getting in the middle or having to worry about hackers being able to get a hold of their information.

Even if you are not interested in some of the benefits of cryptocurrencies, there is still a way that you can join. Some people are seeing the potential of these currencies and are choosing to invest in these currencies. This is a great way to make money, as long as you can read the market, learn the signs, and you get in at the right time. This chapter is going to explore some of the simple things that you can do to start investing in cryptocurrencies and see your money grow in no time.

Create a portfolio with only a few cryptocurrencies

As you get into cryptocurrency investing, you will start to create your portfolio. This is going to be pretty much all of the different things that you decide to invest in. For example, with a traditional investment portfolio, you may end up with some stocks, some bonds, some real estate, and so on to fill out the portfolio. This is similar to what you would work on with cryptocurrencies as well. Your portfolio is something that you should always take an active part in creating, and it is something that you will work on for the long term if you really want to see results.

You will want to be a bit different when you are working with a portfolio with cryptocurrencies. While most investment portfolios will recommend that you add in as many different options that you can comfortably handle, it is best if you stick with just two or three different cryptocurrencies at the most.

Cryptocurrencies are very volatile, and they are a new type of investment, so it is often best to just work on a few of them at a time. This helps you to be more selective with your choices, rather than just picking out all of them and stretching yourself too thin. You should consider only investing in the currencies that you understand and of course, always keep those emotions under control and your portfolio will grow, even if you only work with a few cryptocurrencies.

Find good, relevant sources

Since these currencies are becoming so popular around the world, there are countless pieces of advice that you can follow that concerns them. You can go to the store and find someone who wants to tell you about the right investment option with cryptocurrencies. You can find a lot of articles online, most o which are full of misleading or false information (they just want to get your money rather than helping you out). Everywhere that you turn, there are a lot of people who promise to give you advice, but most of them are honestly just trying to get your money.

If you want to start investing in these digital currencies, it is best to do your own research. It is nice to talk to someone else about these currencies and get some of their advice, but this is not enough if you want to actually be successful. You have to think for yourself and get the information on your own, and then the success will come.

So, there are a few places you can look to help you out. The first place is to look at the different charts that are available for the currency you would like to work with. You need to look at as many of these charts as possible. Getting a good look at the history of the cryptocurrency, and even some of the more recent trends can help you to make good decisions for investing.

Take some time to look at the news articles that are coming up. Do not just concentrate on the ones that tell you the current news of the coin, such as ones that state that the currency is going up or down. These articles are going to be behind because they will just report the news after it comes or goes. Rather, you need to look at the news and determine how that will affect the currency on your own before the news gets ahold of it. And since these currencies are available all throughout the world, it means that you need to look at the world news as well.

An example of this is with Bitcoin and the Chinese government. Recently the Chinese government announced that they were going to withdraw from this market. If you waited until the news announced this, you would have been surprised by the big drop in value that happened in early September 2017 with Bitcoin. On the other hand, if you had been following the news for a few months before this, you would have been aware that China was planning on developing their own form of cryptocurrency to bolster their economy, and you could have prepared for this.

It is also a good idea to talk to someone who has worked inside the cryptocurrency market for some time. You do have to be a discerning investor and decide what advice is good to follow and which advice is bad for you, but it never hurts to talk to someone who is already in the market. This will help you to get a good idea of what is going on in the market and provides you with some insider tips that you may not be able to find anywhere else. Try to find a few professionals you can talk with, so you get a good feel for investing in the cryptocurrency market.

Most cryptocurrencies will not last

As a beginner investor, you have to realize that most of the cryptocurrencies that are on the market are not going to last, which makes them a horrible idea to work with. A few options, such as Bitcoin, LiteCoin, and Ethereum, have become really popular and are used all throughout the world. But because they are so popular, there are hundreds of these digital currencies that are popping up all over the place. Most of them do not have the staying power to last, and choosing to go with them could leave you losing your money.

When we are looking at cryptocurrencies, we are seeing a lot of dotcom hype that is arising around them, which means that we can assume that about 80 percent of these cryptocurrencies are not going to be able to survive the long term. This is something similar to what happened with all of the dotcom hype. The reason for this is that during all of this hype, the investors and the users are not focusing enough on the real added value that these currencies are creating.

It is imperative for you to realize what kind of value these digital currencies are providing before you decide to invest in them. They need to be able to withstand the test of time, provide some value to the user, and be able to keep on going, even when all of the hype is gone. There are a lot of little companies who are trying to make their own digital currencies right now, but it is unlikely that they will stick around and they are a waste of your money.

Check on the market cycle

Another place that you can check out when working with investing in cryptocurrencies. More precisely, you want to make sure that you know where you are in the market cycle. The market cycle is going to determine when you make purchases and when you sell the investment that you have to make the most profit. If you are on the wrong end of the market cycle when you make purchases or sales, you will lose out.

On every investment, there is going to be a high point and a low point. You want to make sure that you are purchasing or buying into the currency when the market cycle is at a low point because this means you are getting a good deal in the process. On the other hand, when the market cycle reaches the high point, or close to the high point, you want to make a sale because this is when the investment reaches a high price. The close you are to both of these points at the right time, the more profit you will make.

You have to always look at the market cycle before you make purchases though. If you happen to do this wrong and make a purchase when the market is at a high point, you are going to be in trouble. The market may go up a little, but it is likely to go back down again before you can sell. Even if you are successful at selling again before it goes down, you will miss out on a good deal of profit along the way.

In addition, you never want to sell when you are at a low point. This means that the current demand for the investment is low and if you choose to sell right now, you are going to end up losing money. It is likely that you purchased the stock at a much higher price and most people who end up selling during one of the downturns in the market cycle do so because they are worried about losing even more money. But you have to wait out the cycles because it will go back up and you will earn a profit.

So, your next question is probably how do you tell where you are in the market cycle. This can be a bit of a challenge if you do not go through and look at some research. The first thing that you need to do is get ahold of some graphs for whichever digital currency you would like to work with. These charts should have information about how the value of that currency has gone up and down since the beginning.

You will want to take a look at how the stock has been doing since it was released because this can help you to figure out if there are any patterns that go on with that currency. It may not be completely regular, but there is often a pattern present that makes it easier to tell about how much time goes on between each part of the market cycle. Perhaps each week it changes; one week it goes up to a high point, and the next week it goes down and so on.

Another thing to look for is the mean between each of the high points and the low points and see if there is an average that occurs. You may have one mean that is at $5 with the high being seven and the low being three. Then the next time the mean is $10 with the high being $13 and the low being $7. You can figure out what the percentage change is between each part and use that to figure out how it may change while you are in the market.

These charts are going to help you to figure out where you are in the market. If you take a look and notice that you are getting near a low point according to the information that you have already seen from the past, now is the time to jump into the market because you are going to get a good deal. On the other hand, if you notice that the char seems to be reaching a high point, it is best to wait a bit, so you do not end up losing money.

This can also help you when it is time to sell your currency. If you purchased at a low point, you would be able to use the charts and watch the market, to figure out what time will be best to sell the stocks and earn the most money. You do not have to wait until the exact top point (and doing so can actually make you lose money), but it will help you to pull out of the market at a place that is comfortable for you while still making a profit.

Learn the potential: many people have yet to hear of cryptocurrencies

One thing that is really unique with these digital currencies is that, even though they have been out for a bit of time now, there is still a lot of potential for how much it can grow. There are still a ton of people who have never even heard about these digital currencies, which means as the market grows, there are still quite a few people who will be able to join in on the fun as well. And the bigger the market (or, the more people who join the network), the more your coins will be worth.

It is important for you to take some time to look at the real world usage when you are trying to decide whether you would like to invest in these digital currencies. The good news here is that most analysts believe that what has happened with these currencies so far is just the beginning.

According to Statista, the number of adults throughout the United States who are even familiar with Bitcoin (which is the most known digital currency right now), is only at 24 percent. In addition, the number of those that actually use Bitcoin in America right now is merely 2 percent, while about 25 percent talk about perhaps using this kind of currency in the future.

These numbers should excite you as an investor. This isn't just true when we talk about Bitcoin, but it is even truer when we talk about the other digital currencies. This means that there is a lot of great potentials when it comes to how these coins will be used in the future. We just looked at the numbers of those who do not know about or do not use these currencies in America right now but think of all the people you could reach all throughout the world.

And as more of these people start to join the network, it means that you have more value for these coins over time.

As an investor, it is always good news to hear that your investment is going to grow in the future, and right now is a great time to jump on before that value goes up.

Be prepared for the losses

This one is going to be hard for beginners to stomach when they first get started. They may have been told by their friends and other professionals that the best investment ever was to get into digital currencies and they were so excited to get all of this started. They may have planned out for a few weeks to figure out how the market works and how they can get started. But then the unthinkable happens, they end up losing on the investment they made.

The digital currency market is really volatile, which means that it has a lot of big ups and big downs. While this can result in you earning a lot of good money in the process, it also adds the risk. Most beginners will choose to go with a stock that is steadier. One that has a steady upward trend, but does not have the crazy ups and downs. These digital currencies have not reached that point yet, which means they can be pretty risky.

What this means for you is that you have to be prepared to receive some losses. You have to really learn how to read this market and even people who have been working on it for some time are finding that it is hard with all of the fluctuations that keep occurring. Make sure that you feel really comfortable with your research methods, that you learn how to read the market, and that you only invest the amount of money that you are comfortable with losing and you will do much better with your investment.

Figure out your strategy and stick with it

When it comes to investing in digital currencies, you have a few different strategies that you can work with, and all of them can be successful. The trick is that you pick out one strategy and then stick with it no matter what. One of the worst things that you can do is skip from one strategy to another and get things mixed up. Of course, if you try out a strategy for a bit and find that it is not working that great for you or you do not like it, it is just fine to switch off and try another one. But when you are in the middle of a trade, never think about switching strategies, or you will lose out on your money.

There are a few different strategies that you can use. One popular method is the buy and hold strategy. This method does not require a lot of work from you as the investor other than a good understanding of the market and the ability to make good estimations of where the market is going in the future.

With the buy and hold method, you will purchase some of the coins, and then you will just hold onto them for a few months or more. This is a long-term investment option because it requires you to wait until the value of the coin goes up. From day to day, the value of each cryptocurrency is going to go up and down, as is pretty normal with any option that is as volatile as these coins. But the good news is that over the long-term, these coins have seen an upward trend. As more and more people discover what these coins are about and decide to jump into the market, the value is sure to go up.

Let's look at an example of this. In February of 2017, the value of Bitcoin got t about $2500 per coin. By August 2017, the value of Bitcoin got up to about $4800 a coin. If you had held onto the coins for just six months and then exchanged them out for your traditional currency and you would have made a good profit. You do need to have a plan for this one, such as how long you will hold onto the coins and when you will decide to leave the market or cut your losses, but it can be effective, and relatively easy method to make money on this market.

Some investors choose to go with day trading. This will require you to make a lot of small trades throughout the day, purchasing the coins when they are lower in value and then selling them when there is a slight increase in prices. This option is more of a short-term option, relying n on the constant fluctuations that come with these currencies. The important thing to remember though is that you need to make the trades all in one day, both the purchases and the sales and that this needs to be done before you go to sleep that night. These currencies are available all throughout the world, and if you do not make your sales before you go to sleep that night, there could be some major fluctuations that you do not know about in other parts of the world, and you may lose out on a lot of money.

These are just two of the strategies that you can consider when it comes to investing in cryptocurrencies. Each strategy can be successful, but you have to know how they are going to work and you have to make sure that you are sticking with the one that you choose. If you can do this, you are much more likely to be successful.

Invest what you can afford

No matter what you are investing in, you must make sure that you never invest in more money than you would be comfortable losing if things go bad. Even the best investors have times when the market does not go the way that they want, and they can lose out on a lot of money in the process. With the cryptocurrency market being so new and volatile, it is sometimes hard to predict where things will go and there are times when you could lose money on your investment.

Many beginners get excited about the market. They are ready to jump right into the opportunity because they have heard a lot of news about this kind of currency. Someone may have given them a tip about one of these currencies, so they are excited about getting started. But in this excitement, they do not spend time doing the right research to figure out what will work the best for them. They may not see that the market is still volatile, that it does have some ups and downs, and if they are not careful, they could still lose out on everything.

You need to figure out what you are the most comfortable with losing. It is possible that you will lose money in this process, and if you took out your retirement fund, all your savings, and more, you could be in some trouble, especially as a beginner who does not understand how the market is supposed to work. Never invest so much that you would be in financial ruins if you lost it all.

As a beginner, it is best if you set aside a little bit of savings, some "fun" money that you can use however you would like and that would not be the end of the world if you ended up losing it. You can invest in the market and hopefully make some good choices so that you earn money back. With this option, you are comfortable if you lose the little bit of money, but you could still earn a big profit. No, you are not going to earn as much as you could if you put everything that you had towards the investment, but at least you will not lose as much either.

Many people decide that cryptocurrencies are the best ways for them to start investing their money. They are excited for the change to earn an income on these currencies, which seem to be going up all of the time. With the help of these great tips, you can go from a beginner to an expert in cryptocurrency investing in no time.

Chapter 2: Trading in Cryptocurrency

One option that you can work with when it comes to cryptocurrencies is to trade in them. Once you find a good exchange site that you can use that has the features that you like and will not charge a lot in fees for each transaction, it is pretty easy to start trading in these currencies. Of course, you will also need to make sure that you have some traditional currency ready to go to help you out.

Many people think that trading in these digital currencies should be an easy way to make money and they are partly right. These are easy compared to some of the other options that are out there, such as penny stocks and binary options, but that does not mean there isn't an element of risk and challenge to each trade. You have to have some goals in place, be able to chart how your success is going, and even learn how to keep your emotions in place, so they do not stop your progress. Not everyone is cut out to work with digital currency trading, even if it sounds easy on paper.

This chapter is going to take a look at some of the things that you need to do if you would like to see success with trading in cryptocurrencies. This type of trading can be difficult at times, but with the right attitude and the right tips, you will be able to get it all done.

Set goals that are realistic

Before you decide to trade in cryptocurrency, you need to make sure that you set some goals and that they are realistic. Because of the big increases in value that have occurred with Bitcoin in the past few years, there are a lot of people who are excited about jumping on this opportunity, and they may set up some goals that are cray to follow.

Yes, there are times when these cryptocurrencies are going to see big leaps in value, especially as more and more people find out about them and because they are still so new. But setting goals that are based on these crazy increases will just lead you to failure. They will force you to make bad decisions with your investment and then when the downturn does happen, which it easily could at any time, you will end up failing.

Setting realistic expectations as a beginner is the key to success, and it will help you to determine what strategy you want to go with. If you want to make this into a part-time income, you can then determine which strategy will be able to help you reach that goal. But if you want to use this for your retirement plan, to go on vacation, or as a way to replace your full-time income, your strategy is going to be different.

To help you stay on course, it is a good idea to write down the goals that you want to meet. These can change over time, but the point here is to have something solid, something that is written down, that you can take a look at any time that you are lost for what to do, or you wonder if you want to stick with the plan. You can make the goals anything that you want, as long as they are realistic goals that you can actually follow and as long as they will keep you accountable.

The Buy and Hold strategy

Probably one of the most effective trading options when it comes to working with cryptocurrencies, especially for beginners, is the buy and hold strategy. This strategy does not require a lot of work from you, outside of being able to watch the market and decide when it is a good time to purchase and when it is a good time to sell your coins.

The idea of the buy and hold strategy is that you are trying to purchase the coins when they are at a low and then you will sell them when they reach a high. Some people just hold onto the coins for a certain amount of time, others will sell them once they reach a certain amount of profit, and some just keep them there because they haven't decided how to use them yet. This is a long-term investment strategy though which means that you will need to hold onto the coins for at least a few months to see the results.

To get started with this method, you simply need to join the network that you want to use, setting up an account, a wallet, and whatever else they require of you. You can then find an exchange site that will help you take your traditional currencies and trade them in for some of the currency that you would like. There are many exchange services available, and the one that you choose is going to depend on the currency that you want to work with.

Once you have your currencies, you will be able to put them into your wallet and hold onto them. Since this is a long-term strategy, which means you will not be using the coins for a few months or more, you will need to consider moving the coins to a safe location. Leaving the coins online, especially when you do not plan to use them, leaves them susceptible to a hacker getting ahold of them. Cold storage such as moving it to your hard drive or printing off your private key will help you to keep the coins safe while you wait.

After a few months have passed, or you earn a certain amount depending on what strategy you were working with, you will decide to trade the currency back out. You will end up with a profit if everything went right, but you will have it back in your traditional currency.

This method has been extremely successful. For example, when Bitcoin was first started, each coin was barely worth a few dollars each. This was in 2009. As of writing this book, the value of each coin was worth over $4000 each. This would be a huge increase if someone had held onto their coins for that long.

Of course, most people probably did not hold onto their coins from 2009 since investing in cryptocurrency was not that popular back then. Still, there has been a big increase in the value in the last few months. In February of 2017, the value of Bitcoin was around $2500. Then in August, it reached a new high of over $4800. You would have only had to hold onto your coins for about six months, and you could have earned a huge profit in the process for very little work.

Before joining in on this kind of investment, please do your research. You need to make sure that you are joining a stable cryptocurrency, one that will continue to go up and will not fail or go out of business while your coins are inside. Most cryptocurrencies will not see the big increases that were described in Bitcoin, but they do still have some potential as long as you do your research and pick the right ones.

The Day Trading strategy

Another option that you can go with for trading is known as day trading. If you have worked with other stock and investment options, it is likely that you have heard about day trading at some point. It is a basic idea, but it does require you to be careful and to understand how the market will go throughout the day. You also will not be able to make a lot of money on each trade, but you will make a bit of money on a lot of trades, so it can add up over time.

With day trading, you are going to purchase the currency and sell it all within the same day. Depending on the fluctuations that happen in the market, you could end up doing this a few times on the same day. The goal is to make a purchase of the currency when the price is as low as possible. Then a few hours later, you will trade the currency back when the value is higher for a profit. If it takes most of the day to complete this, you may only get in one trade. But if the market is really volatile on that day, you may be able to get in a few trades that day.

There are a few things to watch out for before you start with this method. First, you need to make sure that you understand the market. Just jumping in and hoping for the best will result in you losing money. You have to recognize when you are seeing a low point that day and when you will see a high point so you can maximize your profit. Also, you should keep in mind that each time you trade, you will end up with a small fee from whichever exchange service you are working with so count this in when dealing with your costs.

The biggest thing that you will need to worry about is getting the trades done on time. These cryptocurrencies are used all throughout the world, which means that a lot of fluctuations and price changes can happen when you are asleep. If you do choose to go with day trading, make sure that you finish up all of your sales before you end for the night. This will ensure that nothing big happens at night that jeopardizes your earnings.

Avoid the panic

As a beginner, there are going to be sometimes when the market goes down. You may have just joined the market and are excited about making some money, or you could have been in the market for some time, enjoying the fact that you can make some good money over the long term. Then all of a sudden, the market starts to go down quickly. You lose out on money if you withdraw at this time, and you start to feel worried.

The beginner is likely to go through one of these fluctuations, and they will withdraw all of their money all at once. They will decide that it is better to take the loss, but often this is just a temporary downturn. Is it really worth taking a loss on a trade just because the market went down for an hour or two? This may seem a little bit silly, but it is something that a lot of beginners will end up doing.

This is a good lesson in leaving your emotions at the door when you are working in cryptocurrencies, and in fact, it can be a valuable lesson no matter what kind of investment you are working on. Once your emotions get into the mix, it becomes almost impossible for you to think through your decisions clearly and you will end up making decisions that will always cause you to lose money.

It is not just with panic or negative emotions where you can end up in trouble as well. Some people have run into trouble when they end up getting excited about what they are doing or the trades that they are working on. They will take a look at the market and see that it just keeps rising again and again. They are so excited about the potential profit that they will receive, so they ignore all of the warning signs and choose to keep on going. Then all of a sudden (or not so suddenly if you were paying attention), the market will go down, and you end up losing out on everything and not making any profit at all.

If you are not someone who can get into an investment and keep a level head, making decisions based on where the market is and where it is going through the research that you do, then trading in cryptocurrency is not the right choice for you. If you are someone who will panic when there are some downturns that make it look like you will lose money, then trading in cryptocurrency is not the right choice for you. If you are easily excitable and will just keep going with things on a whim, despite what the research and all the professionals are telling you, then trading in cryptocurrency is not the right choice for you.

The best way to make sure that you will avoid the panic or any of the other emotions that can ruin all your hard work and potential profits is to make sure that you have a plan in place. This would include a strategy that you would like to use, an enter and exit strategy, and other things that will keep you on track, no matter how the market is doing. But for those who are not able to handle stressful situations or keep on task, investing in cryptocurrency is probably not the best option for them.

Never use guesswork

Have you been taking a look at the cryptocurrency market lately, looking at how it has been doing and kind of watching out the market goes up and down? If so, you have probably noticed that the digital currency market is really crazy and it is hard to predict what is going to happen from time to time. This is often true because it is so new and there are still a lot of people who are trying to join the network at any given time. And since these markets are available all throughout the world, fluctuations are going to happen based on a lot of countries.

Because of all these changes and fluctuations, it is important to take the guesswork out of the mix. Even as an experienced investor, it is never a good idea to try to anticipate where the market will go in the future. There are some investors who will go and make decisions based on hunches, but the smart ones will still do their homework and some research before they try to take action.

Never go into a trade without doing as much homework as possible ahead of time. Yes, there are a lot of times when the market is going to go a different way than you would like. But often, doing some research about the market, what is happening around the world, and so much more, can help you to determine where the market will go.

For example, if you find out that a big country is going to all of a sudden leave the market for a particular cryptocurrency, such as what is happening with China and Bitcoin, you will be able to predict that the value of Bitcoin will go down. On the other hand, you may read the news and see that there is a new country that is going to allow more freedom in the market or takes off some of their regulations against cryptocurrencies, you could estimate that the value will go up.

These markets are still very volatile because they are brand new and because they are relying on factors from all over the world rather than on just what is going on in one country. But with some research, you can take out some of the guesswork and can increase your chances of making money with cryptocurrencies.

When mistakes are made, learn from them

To be honest, as a beginner you are going to make some mistakes along the way. There are going to be things that you do wrong at some point. You may not take a look at the market cycle, you may put in more money than you really should to the market, you may make decisions on momentary fluctuations of the market and many other issues that can make you lose out on money.

Even those who have been in the market for some time can make mistakes. It is nothing to be ashamed of to make mistakes. Yes, you may end up losing some money in the process. But the biggest issue with these mistakes is that you may not try to learn from them. If you end up making a mistake, try to learn from it as much as possible. Try to figure out how to avoid that mistake again, how you could have done things differently to avoid that mistake in the future and anything else that you can.

One trick that you can try to do is to write down the different trades that you are working on and how they turn out. It does not matter if you were successful with the trade or you ended up failing, make sure that you write all the information down. This may seem like a big waste of time, but if you are ever unsure about what you should do on a particular trade sometime in the future, you can always go back through your notes and learn from what you did in the past.

You are going to make some mistakes along the way. You can stay in the market too long, you can decide that you want to switch strategies in the middle of a trade, or a million other things. But if you realize that you made a mistake and you learn from that mistake, you will be able to see much better results in no time.

Chart how you are doing

You should never just go into your investment without having a chart of how your investment is doing. There are going to be some up and down movement when it comes to the different digital currencies, but you need to decide on your choices based on how the currency is doing over the long term.

As a beginner, you may find that it is easy to concentrate on how the market is doing from one day to the next, or even from one hour to the next. There are going to be sometimes when the market is going to go down, and there may be a week or two where the market is below what you would like. This can scare some people because they want to make money off their investment.

If you are only focusing on the short term, which is easy to do if you do not have a chart in place of your currency, you are going to make bad decisions for your investment. You will join the market or leave the market based on some fluctuations that are pretty momentary, rather than on the trends in the market. This is why it is always a good idea, no matter where you are investing your money but especially with cryptocurrencies, that you make purchases and sell based on the long-term data.

Love thy crypto

When you are working with some of the traditional methods of trading, they can be pretty dry and boring. You may choose an option because it seems to make a lot of money, maybe low at risk, or has another benefit that you like the best. But you rarely are going to pick out an option because you think it is a passion of yours. This is usually the safest way to invest your money, but it can make investing kind of boring.

On the other hand, working with cryptocurrencies do not have to be this way. You can add in some passion when you are working with digital currencies. Of course, you should not choose to go with cryptocurrencies just because you think that they are a get rich quick scheme, but you can still have some passion for what you are doing. Many people who invest in this kind of currency like to do it because they like the principles and the concepts behind the currency that they pick.

And this brings up another point that you need to concentrate on. You need to make sure that you really understand what you are doing with each cryptocurrency that you pick. There are some that are pretty similar, but they do have some different principles and concepts behind them. If you just get into a currency because you think that it will make you money, without understanding how the currency actually works, you will end up becoming bored with this investment strategy.

As we mentioned before, you should only pick two or three currencies that you want to add to your portfolio. This is a good idea because it helps you to really concentrate on them and you can do your research. When you love the currencies that you are working with, investing in them can be more fun, and you will end up making more money.

Decide on your exit strategy

Going into your trade without a plan is one of the worst things that you can do when it is time to make some money with these currencies. There are too many beginners who will go into the market and assume that a plan of "make as much money as possible" is going to help them out. Yes, there are a lot of people who have gotten lucky and have made a lot of money trading when the market jumps up a lot, but you need to have a plan in place. This helps to reduce your risk so you make as much as possible while limiting how much you could potentially lose.

The first thing that you need to decide is how much money you are willing to lose. If the worst case scenario happens and you end up losing money, how much would you be comfortable with losing before you started to panic? There are going to be some fluctuations in the price and just because it goes down a little bit does not mean the price will not go back up. But there are also times when the price will continue to go down, and if you stay on the market, you are going to lose out on a lot of money.

For this part of the exit strategy, you need to decide how much you would be fine with losing. Once the market reaches that point, it is time to pull out. Yes, there are going to be times when the market will go back up, and you may feel bad when you missed out because you didn't stay in long enough. But there are going to be plenty of times when the market keeps going down, and you will be thankful for getting out before you lost even more money. The good news is that you can save yourself a lot of loss and you can always get back into the market again if it goes back up.

On the other side of things, you also need to have an exit strategy for when you will have earned enough money, and you are ready to get out. Some beginners want to just keep going so they can make a ton of money, but this is a risky strategy as well. If you just keep riding the market, you may make more if you are lucky, but you could also run into the issue of the market turning down really quickly, which often happens when you reach big highs, and you could lose all your money and more.

Some people have trouble with this part of the strategy. They may understand having an exit strategy when the market is low because it helps to protect them, but they do not understand why they would want to leave the market early when they are making money. It is really just a way to protect you and make sure that you do not end up losing out on money if the market suddenly takes a turn. Yes, you may lose out on some profit if the market does keep going up, but you will still make some money, and you can always join in later.

So, before you decide to join the market, decide how much you would like to earn or would be the right return on investment for your needs. When the market gets to this point, you will decide to leave and take the profits. Then you can wait until the market goes through the right cycle again and you can join later on.

Trading in cryptocurrency is a good way to make money, but it can be a little bit tricky for a beginner to start with. Trading in cryptocurrency is not going to be like some of the other stocks and options that you may choose to go with, mostly because it is brand new and the market is still pretty volatile. But if you follow the tips that are in this chapter, you will become an expert in cryptocurrency trading in no time.

Chapter 3: Mining in Cryptocurrencies

One thing that you can do with cryptocurrencies is to mine. The mining process is a great way to help you to earn more of the coins to use however you would like, whether you use them on the network to make purchases and send money or you exchange them out for some of your traditional currency. This system is going to benefit everyone that is involved. When the miners are successful, they will earn a reward that they can use however they would like. This means that more coins are going to be released into the network for others to use as well, once the miner exchanges them or starts to use them for their own.

And of course, one of the biggest reasons that the mining process is around is because it helps to keep the network safe. The miners will work on complex mathematical equations to keep information about the transactions on that network safe. The users will be able to trust the network more, their information will be secure, and it is more likely that this network will stay around for a lot longer.

In this chapter, we are going to take a look at some of the tips that you need to get started with mining. This is not an easy process to complete, and not everyone has the patience, knowledge, or even the right software and hardware, to get this done. But when you are following some of these tips below, you will find that it can be easy to start out with mining.

Which coins can I mine?

The first thing that we need to look at is what kind of coins you can mine. While there are a lot of different types of digital coins that you can work with, not all of them will allow you to do the mining process. There are a few options that you can choose from and pick the right network can help you figure out how much you will make.

The first coin that you can mine is known as Bitcoin. This is one of the most widely-known online currencies throughout the world, and you can earn up to 25 coins each time that you successfully complete your job. This can be hard, but it is a good reward. However, Bitcoin is not the only option when it comes to your choices for mining. LiteCoin, a coin that is similar to Bitcoin, is easier to get into than Bitcoin, so it is easier for some people to join so there is some value in mining in this coin as well.

Of course, LiteCoin and Bitcoin are not the only two options that you can choose for mining. There are dozens of cryptocurrencies that are available for you to use, including dogecoin. Dogecoin may not be worth near as much as some of the bigger ones on the market, and some people may choose to turn away from it, the return on investment with some of these currencies have a larger chance of being successful.

Out of all the cryptocurrencies that you can choose to mine, Bitcoin is probably one of the best known, perhaps because it is one of the oldest. Many other digital currencies will use the same kind of framework and reward system as Bitcoin, so as a beginner this could be a good one to get started on. Remember, the reward is high for being able to mine in these digital currencies, which means that the work is going to be tough and there is going to be a lot of competition along the way. Mining is not meant to be the easy way to earn coins, but if you are up to working on the algorithms and you have the right computer setup, it can be an option for you.

What hardware do I need?

To get started with mining, you do need to make sure that you have a few things in place. When Bitcoin, one of the fist cryptocurrencies to be developed, was launched during 2009, it was possible for you to use your regular computer to mine the coins. The process of solving the required mathematical equations could be done by the CPU of your computer, so anyone on the network was able to get this work done.

However, over the past few years, the difficulty of mining on this network got more difficult, and it is now impossible to mine with the help of a CPU. Instead, users needed some extra power to accomplish this goal, and most will need to use a GPU or a graphical processing unit.

From here, it became more of a competition as the miners worked to produce computers that were more powerful that had rows of graphics cards to do the work. If you want to be able to create your own mining machine or you are purchasing one, you need to remember that it should be bulked up with some extra GPU's. These can be very demanding on the amount of power that you have. Since you are going to run several graphics cards at the same time, you have to have the right type of power so that your system will remain stable and running while you do the work.

So, what does this mean that you need to get started? You are going to need a computer that is a little more advanced than a regular type of computer to make this happen. You have to remember there are some serious computer programmers out there who are working with mining as well and you need to compete with them if you want to earn money.

First, you will need to make sure that you have your basic motherboard. In addition, you should try to get as many graphics cards as you can to make the computer have as much power as possible. Of course, add in a good hard drive, although you do not necessarily need to store the mined coins on your hard drive if you do not want to. From here, you should be ready to get started with the hardware portion that you need.

What software do I need?

In addition to making sure that you have the right hardware to handle all of the power for your mining experiences, you also need to make sure that the right software is in place. To accomplish mining, you need to make sure that you can solve some complex mathematical equations to earn the coins. The right software can make this process easier.

As the mining rig will have been assembled from scratch, you will need to go through and install the right kind of operating system. Many computers will work with Windows, and while this one may work fine for a lot of other computer processes, this software is not the best for working with cryptocurrency mining. Some people in the Bitcoin community actually find that Windows systems pose a lot of security risks and that it should not be trusted.

A better operating system to go with for this process is to use Linux. There are a few options that have been developed that are optimized for mining such as LinuxCoin and BAMT. The first one is going to only work with the LiteCoin currency, but both do have some mining software that is included right inside of the operating system.

If you want to look for some other types of mining software, whether you place to work with Mac, Linux, or a Windows operating system, visit Bitcoin's page. It is set up kind of like a Wikipedia page where you can find all kinds of good information including some good mining software that you can work with.

Once you have figured out the operating system that you like and a good mining program is installed, it is time to pick out the wallet software that you want to use. As you go through and mine your coins, you need to have someplace where you can store these coins. You are not able to store these coins on some pieces of data, like what you do with your digital picture. Instead, you are going to store the encryption keys that will allow sole access the coins. So, instead of having your hard drive store 100MB of Bitcoins (or however many of these coins that you have), you are going to get a private key that you can store and which will tell the trading network what your current balance is, or how many coins belong to you at any given time.

This key is going to be private and will contain a long list of numbers and letters that keeps it separate from any of the other keys on the network. You will be able to store this in your wallet, either online or n your hard drive or you can print it off on your printer to help keep the information safe. You should store the key somewhere that no one else can get ahold of. If you end up losing your key or someone steals it, you will basically lose all access to your coins forever.

Once you have all of this software in place and the hardware on your computer is all set up, the biggest obstacles to starting with mining are out of the way. You will have all that you need to jump into this method and get started. Some people choose to do all of the work themselves, which provides them with a bigger payoff but can be hard because they have to do all of the work and are competing against some of the big companies. Most will decide to join a mining pool to make things a bit easier, and we will discuss this a bit below.

Find a mining pool

As a beginner, one option that you may want to work with is finding a mining pool. Doing all of this work on your own and with your own power from the computer can be a challenge that not everyone is ready to handle. A mining pool is basically a group of miners that will put all of their computing power together to create more of the coins. The main reason that most people will join one of these mining pools is that coins, such as in Bitcoin, will be awarded in bigger blocks, and it is hard to get all of these coins on your own.

When you are working inside of this pool, you will work on some algorithms that are smaller and much easier to solve. You will work on your part of the algorithm and the other people in the pool will work on solving their own. All of this work combined is going to be easier for everyone involved compared to solving the whole algorithm on your own.

With the mining pool, the coins that you earn are going to be shared throughout the pool, based on how much of the algorithm you ended up solving. This method may not provide you with the whole reward, but the pay will be easier to get than doing it on your own, it will help you to make a consistent amount of these coins, and the return on investment will be higher.

You should be careful about the mining pool that you want to join. There are a few different options that you can go with, and you will want to make sure that the option you choose will provide you the most money for your work.

Some of the questions that you should ask before you decide to work on a mining pool include:

- What is the reward method? This would mean how much you will make for your share of the work, how the money is split up, and so on.

- What fees will this mining pool charge in order for you to take your funds out?

- How frequently is this mining pool able to find blocks. This is important because it helps you to know how often you will be rewarded for your work.

- How easy will it be for you to take your own funds out later on

- What states are provided so you can see how well this mining pool is doing?

- Is this pool pretty stable or have they had some trouble getting things up and running?

There are a few different places that you can go to make sure that you are getting the answers to your questions. In terms of working with Bitcoin, you can check out

BitcoinTalk where there are a few threads about this topic or the Bitcoin wiki provides a comparison of the different mining pools for you to take a look at. You can then choose which pool you want to work with, get your username and password, and then you will get to work.

Finding the right mining pool is going to be one of the hardest parts. Each pool wants to make sure that it is picking out the right people; who want to hire someone on who barely does any of the work and causes everyone to lose out on the end results? In addition, you need to make sure that you find a mining pool that will offer the best price for your work, that will be fair in giving you work, and that will actually pay you when the work is done. All of these come together to pose some challenges to those who want to start mining.

Of course, it is just fine if you would like to work on your own during the mining process. There are some people who have seen success with doing this and choose to go with that method. This allows you to earn all of the rewards, but you have to remember that you will also take on all of the risks and have to do all of the work. When you are competing with groups that have many people working and a lot more processing power, you can run into trouble trying to keep up and get the work done because it is just hard to do it all on your own. This is one of the main reasons that people choose to join one of these mining pools if they can find a good one, but the choice is really up to you.

A mining pool may not provide as big of rewards as doing all the work on your own, but you also do not need to work n all of the work on your own. You are more likely to get the blocks to work on, and you only need to work on some of the algorithms. When the block is done, you will be rewarded for your work. This helps you to still earn money, even if you do not have the time, power, or luck to work on some of those long and harder algorithms all on your own.

Use that cold storage for safety

One mistake that most beginners are going to make is that once they receive their new coins, they will choose to store it inside of a wallet online or in another place that is not secure. When you sign up for the Bitcoin network or another cryptocurrency network, you will be able to find a lot of great wallets to work with. Each of them will offer different services or features and people enjoy being able to just have their coins readily available anytime that they want.

There are some issues that come with using these online wallets, or warm storage, to take care of your coins. Hackers are very interested in coming onto this network and stealing the coins if possible. This would make them a lot of money in the process, and if they could hack onto just one wallet, they could get information on hundreds of users. The hacker simply needs to be able to break into the database of your chosen wallet, and they can get what they want. Once a hacker gets ahold of this information, there are hundreds of users, whether they are miners or not, who could lose out on all of their coins.

In addition, there are often errors that can occur with your computer. If you encounter a glitch, or you have a power outage or something else when you are transferring money, you could end up losing out on all of your coins. This is not a good thing, especially when you are working hard to mine these coins, which is why many people choose to work with cold storage instead.

Cold storage is when you take your coins and place them in a wallet that is not online. This can add some more security and makes it harder for something bad to happen. One option is to use your hard drive. You would store your private key on your hard drive, just like you store documents and other important things n your computer.

One thing to remember with this option though is that you need to encrypt the information. There is still the chance that a hacker could go after your personal computer at some point and if you do not add on some encryption and a strong password, they could still get a hold of your information and steal all your coins with the help of your key.

Taking your key off your computer is often seen as the safest option. This is really a good option if you do not plan to use the coins all that often. Some miners like to keep the coins there, earning more and having it there as an investment in case the price goes up. Taking your key offline can help to keep these coins safe. There are a number of options that you can use such as saving the code on a USB drive. Most people who choose this option will print off the key and then store that key someplace secure. Do not just leave the key lying around; if you happen to lose the paper, you lose out on your coins later on.

Often the best thing that you can do to protect your coins is to pick out a few different options for storage. Experts agree that you should have at least two or three places that you are storing your coins, just in case something happens. The more places that your key is securely stored, the harder it will be for the coins to entirely disappear. Backing up your coins on a regular basis, such as each time that you earn more, or you use them, can help keep that key up to date for you.

Storing your coins properly will make it easier for you to use them when you would like. There are a lot of things that could happen, from a computer glitch to a hacker getting a hold of your coins, but if you keep that key secure, all of your hard work mining will not go to waste.

Keep that antivirus up to date

Cryptocurrencies are growing in popularity. They are still relatively new, but as more people find out about these currencies, they are excited to jump on board, and this increases the demand for these coins. Because the demand is going up, the value of these coins, especially in terms of

Bitcoin, are starting to go high, so there is a lot of profit to be made in mining these digital coins.

Because there is so much value that comes with being a miner, there are a lot of hackers who are interested in stealing those coins from you. They want to be able to just empty out your wallet, without having to do all of the work for mining like you did. If you are not careful with what you do on your computer, or you accept emails and other information that are not safe, you could end up losing out on all of your hard-earned money.

As you are working on mining, it is a good idea to make sure that your anti-virus and malware are all up to date. This will help you out in case someone does try to get your currency information. Update this as often as you can and make sure that you go with services that are high-quality; this is not the area where you try to save money, or you could really lose out. Also, you need to do your part as well. Watch the sites that you go on, do not accept emails and invitations from people you do not know, and make sure that you are always careful when you are online.

Mining is a great way for you to earn cryptocurrencies and will keep the network that you are on safe and secure for all of the users. While mining is difficult and can take some time, if you are willing to follow the rules and make sure that you are doing it the right way, it is a fantastic way to join the network, earn some money, and help out others along the way.

Conclusion

Thank for making it through to the end of this book, I hope it was informative and able to provide you with all of the tools you need to achieve your goals for investing, trading and mining cryptocurrencies.

The next step is to decide which method is the right one for your needs to make money with cryptocurrency. Each of the three methods that we talked about in this guidebook can be really successful, but you need to decide which one you would like to work with.

This guidebook discussed cryptocurrencies, and it discussed some of the different ways that you can make money with this method. Making money with cryptocurrencies can be difficult, but it is one of the best ways to earn money, as long as you know the market. This guidebook looked at how to invest, trade, and even mine with the help of these cryptocurrencies.

When you are ready to use cryptocurrencies as your method of investing and making money, make sure to read through this guidebook and refer back to it to help you get started.

Finally, if you found this book useful in any way, a review on Amazon is always appreciated!

www.ingramcontent.com/pod-product-compliance
Lightning Source LLC
Chambersburg PA
CBHW050020230526
45470CB00003B/1054